READING POWER

Technology That Changed the World

The Printing Press
An Information Revolution

Joanne Mattern

The Rosen Publishing Group's
PowerKids Press™
New York

Published in 2003 by The Rosen Publishing Group, Inc.
29 East 21st Street, New York, NY 10010

First Edition

Book Design: Michael DeLisio

Photo Credits: Cover © Ron Watts/Corbis; pp. 5, 8, 11, 14, 15, 16, 17, 19 © Bettmann/Corbis; pp. 6–7 © Corbis; p. 9 © Austrian Archives/Corbis; p. 10 © Hulton/Archive/Getty Images; p. 13 © Historical Picture Archive/Corbis; p. 17 (inset) © Hulton-Deutsch Collection/Corbis; p. 20 Cindy Reiman; p. 21 © Index Stock Imagery

Library of Congress Cataloging-in-Pub

Mattern, Joanne, 1963-
The printing press : an information revolution / Joanne Mattern.
   p. cm. — (Technology that changed the world)
Summary: Presents information on the printing press, including its invention, history, how it works, and how it has affected people's lives.
Includes bibliographical references and index.
ISBN 0-8239-6488-4 (lib. bdg.)
1. Printing—History—Juvenile literature. 2. Printing presses—History—Juvenile literature. [1. Printing—History. 2. Printing presses—History.] I. Title.
Z124 .M356 2003
070.5'09—dc21

                                        2002000527

Contents

Before the Printing Press

People have been printing for thousands of years. In ancient China, Japan, and Korea, people carved words and pictures on wood blocks. Dyes were put on the blocks. Then, the wood blocks were pressed against paper to make an image.

Around the year 1050, movable type was invented by Pi Sheng, a printer in China. This first movable type used single letters that were carved in separate clay tablets, or blocks.

Now You Know

People in Europe did not use movable type until the 1440s.

Pi Sheng's movable type was made out of tablets of baked clay. The tablets could be moved around to make different words.

Pi Sheng

Clay tablets

5

In Europe, monks made most books for church use. Each book was printed by hand. Some books had colorful pictures. The books were expensive and took a long time to make.

Now You Know

A monk worked six days a week and could copy four pages a day. In one year, a monk could copy 1,200 to 1,300 pages.

Gutenberg's Printing Press

In Germany, Johannes Gutenberg invented the first printing press around 1440. Gutenberg's press was made from a machine used to press grapes into wine. In one hour, Gutenberg's press could print about ten sheets of paper.

Gutenberg used his press to print a bible. Gutenberg's Bible is also called The Forty-two-line Bible *because there were 42 lines of type in each column.*

In 1455, a judge ordered Gutenberg to give his printing presses and print shop to a man to whom he owed money.

This is a copy of Gutenberg's first printing press.

Gutenberg used metal movable type in his press. He put ink on the type pieces and lined them up on a flat surface. A sheet of paper was placed over the type. Then a heavy board pressed the paper down onto the type.

In Gutenberg's printing press, each single letter of type had to be placed by hand on an iron tray. This took a lot of time.

The Importance of the Printing Press

The invention of the printing press changed the world. Books could be made faster and cheaper. Writers were able to share their ideas with anyone who could read. Information could now be spread all over the world.

Top Five All-Time Best-Selling Books	Number of Copies
1) *The Bible*	6,000,000,000
2) *Quotations from the Works of Mao Tse-tung*	800,000,000
3) *American Spelling Book* by Noah Webster	100,000,000
4) *The Guinness Book of Records*	81,000,000 [1]
5) *The McGuffey Readers* by William Holmes McGuffey	60,000,000

[1] *Average sales per year*

In 1475, William Caxton set up the first printing press in England.

Advances in Printing

In the 1800s, changes were made to the printing press. In 1812, Friedrich Koenig used a steam engine to make his printing press run faster.

Friedrich Koenig

In 1865, William Bullock invented a press that used long rolls of paper. Bullock's press could print 12,000 newspapers in one hour.

Friedrich Koenig's printing press could print almost four times faster than a hand press.

In 1884, Ottmar Mergenthaler invented the linotype machine. Typesetters could now set type quickly using a keyboard. Typesetting no longer had to be done by hand.

Ottmar Mergenthaler was a German immigrant who lived in Baltimore, Maryland.

The linotype's name came from a comment made by the publisher of the New York Tribune, *Whitelaw Reid* (right). Upon seeing the machine work, Reid said, "Ottmar, you've done it again! A line o' type!"

By the 1950s, metal movable type was replaced by phototypesetting. Phototypesetting uses a light to print images and letters on special paper. The paper is then used in the process of making printing plates. The plates are used in the printing press.

Printing Press Record-Breakers

The largest book, the *Super Book*, measures 9 feet by 10 feet, weighs 557 pounds, and has 300 pages.

The smallest book is a version of "Old King Cole," which measures .04 square inch.

The smallest comic book, *Agent 327*, was published in June 1999. It measures 1 inch by 1.4 inches.

The heaviest issue of a newspaper was the September 14, 1987, edition of *The Sunday New York Times*. It weighed more than 12 pounds and had 1,612 pages.

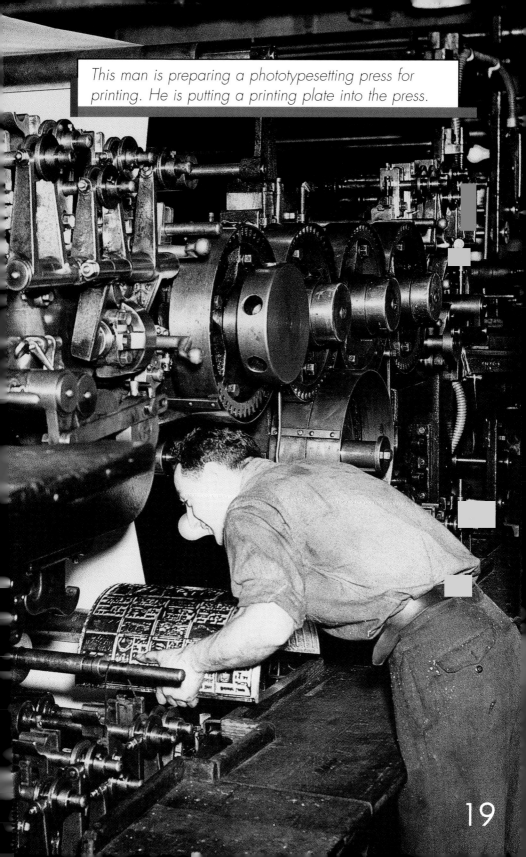

This man is preparing a phototypesetting press for printing. He is putting a printing plate into the press.

The Printing Press Today

In the 1980s, computers began to play an important part in printing. Books and magazines are now typeset on computer screens. The words and pictures are stored on computer disks.

The book that you are reading was typeset using a computer.

Now You Know

In the United States, newspapers sell more than 60 million copies each Sunday. The top ten American magazines sell about 100 million copies a month!

Today, printing presses are so big that they need their own rooms in which to operate. Gutenberg would be surprised to see how much his printing press has been improved.

One roll of newsprint weighs about one ton.

Glossary

carve (**karv**) to cut into something with great care

image (**ihm**-ihj) a picture

linotype (**lyn**-uh-typ) a printing machine that sets type using a keyboard

monk (**muhngk**) a man who is a member of a religious community

movable type (**moo**-vuh-buhl **typ**) single letters that can be moved and grouped as needed to make words

phototypesetting (fo-to-**typ**-seht-ihng) a printing process that uses light, special paper, and film to set type

printing plate (**prihnt**-ihng **playt**) a flat piece of metal with images and type on it, used in printing presses

process (**prahs**-ehs) a way of making something by following a set of steps

technology (tehk-**nahl**-uh-jee) to use knowledge and science to create an easier way of doing something

type (**typ**) a block with a character cut into it that is used in printing

typesetters (**typ**-seht-tuhrz) people who arrange pieces of type into words for books

Resources

Books

Fine Print: A Story About Johann Gutenberg
by Joann Johansen Burch and Kent Alan Aldrich
Carolrhoda Books (1992)

*The Printing Press: A Breakthrough
in Communication*
by Richard Tames
Heinemann Library (2000)

Web Sites

Due to the changing nature of Internet links, PowerKids
Press has developed an on-line list of Web sites related
to the subjects of this book. This site is updated regularly.
Please use this link to access the list:

http://www.powerkidslinks.com/tcw/prpr/

Index

Word Count: 472

Note to Librarians, Teachers, and Parents

If reading is a challenge, Reading Power is a solution! Reading Power is perfect for readers who want high-interest subject matter at an accessible reading level. These fact-filled, photo-illustrated books are designed for readers who want straightforward vocabulary, engaging topics, and a manageable reading experience. With clear picture/text correspondence, leveled Reading Power books put the reader in charge. Now readers have the power to get the information they want and the skills they need in a user-friendly format.